I0777766

# Highland Superstitions

*Druids, Fairies, Witchcraft, Second-Sight, Halloween, Sacred Wells and Lochs.*

*by Rev. Alexander McGregor, M.A.*

**with an introduction by "Black Books"**

*This work contains material that was originally published in 1901.*

*This publication is within the Public Domain.*

*This edition is reprinted for entertainment purposes
and in accordance with all applicable Federal  and International Laws.*

*Introduction Copyright 2017 by Black Books*

# *COVER CREDITS*

### Front Cover
*Tam O'Shanter* by William Carse
[Public domain],
via Wikimedia Commons


### Back Cover
*Auchencar Standing Stone* by © User:Colin
via Wikimedia Commons


### Source
*Wikimedia Commons*
www.Commons.Wikimedia.org

Many thanks to all the incredible photographers,
artists, researchers, and archivists who share and
allow the free use of their great work.


### PLEASE NOTE :
As with all reprinted books of this age that are intended to perfectly reproduce the
original edition, considerable pains and effort had to be undertaken to correct fading and
sometimes outright damage to existing proofs of this title. At times, this task can be quite
monumental, requiring an almost total rebuilding of some pages from digital proofs of
multiple copies. Despite this, imperfections still sometimes exist in the final proof and
may detract slightly from the visual appearance of the text.


### DISCLAIMER :
Due to the age of this book, some methods or practices may have been deemed unsafe or
unacceptable in the interim years.  In utilizing the information herein, you do so at your
own risk.  We republish antiquarian books without judgment or revisionism, solely for
their historical and cultural importance, and for educational purposes.

# Black Books

# NOTE.

THE following pages on "Highland Superstitions," by the late Rev. Alexander MacGregor, M.A., Inverness, first appeared as a series of articles in Volume II. of the *Celtic Magazine*, and subsequently as an appendix to the second, third, and fourth editions of "The Prophecies of the Brahan Seer." They were published separately for the first time in 1891, and now reprinted, 1901.

# CONTENTS

# HIGHLAND SUPERSTITIONS.

IT is lamentable that mankind in all ages of the world have been prone to the most degrading superstitions. The enlightened ages of antiquity were no more exempt from them than the most ignorant. We know from the Bible how difficult it was to restrain the Jews from the most idolatrous and superstitious observances, and to confine them to the worship of the only living and true God. This remarkable tendency of the Hebrew nation was caused, in all likelihood, by their sojourning for the long period of 400 years among the Egyptians, whose system of religion was a mass of idolatrous observances. They had a number of ideal gods, to whom they erected temples of prodigious size and architectural splendour. Their principal deities, were Osiris and Isis, whom they considered typical of the sun and moon. But they had a great variety of other deities, animals of all kinds—(hence the golden calf of the Hebrews),

the dog, the wolf, the hawk, the stork, the cat, and several other creatures. They also adored their great river, the Nile, personifying it in the crocodile, to which they erected temples and appointed priests to serve at their altars. The Egyptians also believed in dreams, lucky and unlucky days, charms, omens, and magic—in short, they were grossly superstitious !

The absurdities of Egyptian superstition formed the basis of what followed in Greece and Rome. Fifteen hundred years before the birth of our blessed Saviour, Egypt was at the height of its civilisation, but then, too, it was at the height of its superstition. The mythology and superstitious observances of the Greeks deserve to be noticed, both as a matter of amusement and instruction, but we can, in the meantime, hint at but a few particulars. They had no idea of the only living and true God. Their notions of Divinity were grovelling and contemptible. Their gods were, as they believed, at one time heroes and rulers on earth, but still having their habitation somewhere within the boundaries of the Grecian territories. We are made acquaint-ed with the character of these imaginary deities by the numer-ous allusions made to them in the works of the Greek and Roman poets, as well as by the various sculptured figures which have been brought to light in modern times. Jupiter, the son of Saturn, was the chief God. But even the great Jupiter himself did not enjoy unmolested his supreme dignity, for the offspring of Titan, a race of terrible giants, set Jupiter at defiance. They piled the mountains of Pelion and Ossa on the top of each other, and endeavoured to ascend into heaven, and to pull Jupiter down from his throne. The gods, in great alarm, fled from Mount Olympus into Egypt, where they concealed their true character by assuming the form of various animals; but Jupiter, assisted by Hercules, succeeded in destroying the giants, and in reasserting his sovereign sway. And hence he is always represented on a throne, with a thunderbolt in his hand, and an eagle by his side. Jupiter's brothers and children were the gods and goddesses of a great variety of distinct things—in fact, under the complicated mythology of Greece, every imaginable thing had its god or goddess. For example, Jupiter's brother Neptune was god of the ocean, and is painted as a majestic figure, with a crown on his head, and a trident in his hand, and drawn in a car over the sea by powerful water-horses. Neptune has often appeared in his stately chariot on the decks of ships when crossing the Equator. Then all on board who had never crossed the line before were brought into his presence, laid hold of, and plunged into a bath of water, where they received a smart shave, with tar for soap, and a rusty hoop for a razor. Only the ladies on board were exempted from this unpleasant treatment, not because they had no beards, but by the powerful talismanic effect of slipping a few sovereigns into the hands of the seamen for grog.

The superstitions of the European Northmen, or Scandinavians (the early inhabitants of Denmark, Norway, Sweden, and Iceland), were of a kind remarkably accordant with the cold and stern character of the regions which they occupied. The dread names of their gods Odin, Thor, and other deities of the north are now only perpetuated in the names given to some of the days of the week. Thus, our term "Wednesday" is derived from "Oden's" or Woden's" day— the day of the week on which the northern Jupiter was specially worshipped. Our Thursday is from Thor, the second dignity among the fabulous gods. As this day was called " Dies Jovis " by the Romans, we have a confirmation that Thor, the thunderer, was equivalent to the thundering

Jove of the Grecian mythology.  Friday takes its name from Freya, the beautiful daughter of Niord, and corresponds with the " Dies Venevis," or " Venus-day " of the Greeks and Romans.  Saturday is derived in the same manner from the god " Saeter " of the Scandinavians, or Saturn of the Greeks.  Tuesday, or anciently " Tiesday " (a pronunciation still preserved in many parts in Scotland), is from " Tisa," the wife of Thor; Sunday and Monday were named from the sun and moon, both by the northern and southern nations of Europe, from a remote period.

DRUIDISM.—Interesting as are the ancient superstitions of Greece, Rome, and the northern regions of Europe, we feel a greater interest in the history of Druidism, the great super-stition which flourished peculiarly among our own forefathers, the aboriginies of the British Islands.  Druidism was the religion of the ancient Celts or Gauls, and prevailed in France, and everywhere, indeed, wherever that ancient race had formed settlements.  Several learned inquirers into the native Druidism have cavilled much about the etymology of the word.  Some writers, as Pliny, derive " Druidh " from the Greek " Drus " an oak ; but we think that the proper etymon is the ancient Celtic vocable, " Drù " an oak tree, from which no doubt " Drus " was taken.  The Druids, we believe, had their name before the Greek language was in existence, and it is well known that the Greek itself is partly at least of Celtic origin.  As far as can be gathered from the statements of Cæsar, Diodorus Siculus, Strabo, and others, the Druids not only formed the priesthood of the Celts, but appointed to themselves all the offices now usually discharged by the several learned professions.  There appears to have been three orders among their priests—the Druids proper, the Vates, and the Bards—who severally performed different functions.    The Bards sung, in heroic verse, the brave actions of eminent men; the Vates studied the productions of nature and the laws; while the Druids directed the education of youth, and officiated in the affairs of religion and justice. In their hands they commonly carried a long wand, and their arms and necks were decorated with golden chains and bracelets.    But the most notable of their ornaments was an artificial egg set in gold, and of miraculous virtues.    They asserted that every one of these eggs, which they sold at enormous prices, was formed by a number of serpents, mysteriously conjoining for its production.    When made, it was raised up in the air by the hissing of these reptiles, and was to be caught in a clean white cloth when falling to the ground.    The person who was fortunate enough to catch it had instantly to mount a swift horse, and escape from the angry serpents.    Procured in this way, the egg possessed the property of making the owner successful in all his under-takings.    The open sky was the canopy under which they worshipped.    A wood or grove, fenced in by large stones, constituted the scenes where their rites were performed.    In the centre of the groves was an open area, encompassed by large, erect stones, closely set together.    Here there were circles within circles, and in the centre of the inner one there was a stone of prodigious size, on which the victims were slain, and offered up to the Supreme Being.    The fruit of the oak, and especially the mistletoe bough, were thought to possess a divine virtue.    The mistletoe is perhaps one of the most remarkable parasitic plants in the world, hence it became an object of superstitious regard.    It grows chiefly on the oak and chesnut.    It is an evergreen, and appears strange in winter, with its brilliant green leaves on an otherwise leafless tree.    It is thought that it springs from a seed carried by birds from tree to tree, landed in a crevice:

of the bark, where it sprouts, and derives its nourishment from the living wood, like a graft in a fruit tree. The mistletoe bough grows sometimes as large as a bushel basket—sometimes four or five feet in diameter—of a roundish form, and covered with leaves of the brightest green. Two white bulls were brought and fastened to a tree by the horns, then the arch-Druid ascended the tree, cropped the mistletoe with his golden knife, and received it in his robe, amid the shouts of the people. Then the bulls were sacrificed on the large stone, and the deity was invoked to bless the gift. The Druids had an idol of gigantic size, formed of wicker-work in the rude likeness of a human being. They filled it with human victims, men and women. Straw and wood were piled around it, and the unfortunate creatures within perished in the flames by a slow, horrible death. It is said by some historians that women were more frequently the victims of these superstitious cruelties than the men. Young, innocent, beautiful maidens were dragged to the altar, and sacrificed to the powers above.

Many Druidical relics still exist. By far the most extraordinary of these remains are those at Stonehenge, on Salisbury plain, in Wiltshire. They are numerous on the Western Isles, and some are near Inverness, such as the relics at Clava, on Nairnside, and the circles at Strathnairn and at Culduthel. Mona, or Anglesea, as it is now called, was their chief settlement; but it is in North Britain that the Druidical monuments are most abundant. As a specimen of a Druidical cairn, we may mention that on the Moor of Strathardle, in Perthshire—a stoney mound, ninety yards in circumference, and twenty-five feet high. Such monuments are numerous along the Grampian range. There are also curious stones, called rocking-stones, supposed to be of Druidical origin. In the parish of Kells, in the

Stewartry of Kirkcudbright, there is a rocking-stone called the " Logan-stone," about ten tons in weight ; and it is so nicely balanced upon another stone that the pressure of a child's hand can set it in motion.  A similar stone may be seen on the glebe of the parish of Strath, in Skye.  The artifices of the Druids to deceive the ignorant were numerous. For example, among the ancient Britons a meteor was supposed to be a vehicle for carrying to paradise the soul of some departed Druid.  So well did they engraft their absurd ideas on the minds of the ignorant, that, even at this distant day, the appearance of a ball of fire, meteor, or of what are called falling stars, creates, among the more credulous Highlanders, a belief that some illustrious spirit has taken its flight to eternity.  From this circumstance we may infer, with Dr. Smith, that " Dreug," the Gaelic for a meteor, is a contraction for " Druidh-eug "—a Druid's death.  This ingenious antiquarian thinks that this Druidical fantasy had its origin in a tradition of Elijah's fiery chariot.  While Druidical superstitions were at one time prevalent over the continent of Europe and the adjacent Isles, their extinction is enveloped in the mystery of the dark ages.  Up to a late period, however, some traces of Druidical customs were perceivable among the Scottish Celts.  Dr. Jamieson mentions that an old Highlander, so lately as the end of the eighteenth century, was in the habit of addressing the Deity by the title of Arch-Druid.

Dr. Smith says that the British Druids owed their decline to the following circumstances :—Trathal, the grandfather of Fingal, being chosen generalissimo of the Caledonian army sent against the Romans, did not feel disposed, on his return, to resign his authority, even at the command of the Druids; hence arose a civil war, in which the army of the church was defeated in several battles.  These overthrows were fatal to the Druids.  They made several attempts to regain their dominions, but all were ineffectual.  They retired tc the I-thonn (the isle of waves), that is Iona, where their order was not quite extinct on the arrival of St. Columba on that island, in the sixth century.

FAIRIES.—Among the various spiritual beings to whom the credulity of mankind has given an imaginary existence, the fairies occupy a prominent place, and are specially worthy of notice.  The fairy is distinguished by one peculiarity from every other being of a similar order.  Other spirits, such as dwarfs, brownies, elves, and such like, are represented as deformed creatures, whereas the fairy is a beautiful miniature of " the human form divine ".  It is perfect in face, delightful in  figure, and more of angelic than human appearance.   These points of distinction, with generally a dress of bright green, mark the personal individuality of the fairy. The origin of the fairy superstition is ascribed to the  Celtic race ; hence in Ireland, the Highlands and  Islands of Scotland, and Wales, the fairies are even  to this day believed by some to exist.  They were usually called "good neighbours," " Daoine-sithe," men of peace, and yet, if offended, they became very inveterate in their spite.  They readily kidnapped unbaptised children, and even adult men and women, particularly young married females, to  become nurses to the fairy children.  They lived under ground, or in little green hills, where the royal fairies held their courts.  In their places all was beauty and splendour.  Their pageants and processions were far more magnificent than any that Eastern sovereigns could get up or poets devise.  They rode upon milk-white steeds.  Their dresses were brilliant beyond conception, and when they mingled in  the dance, their music was more sublime by far than mortal lips or hands could ever produce.

The fairy legends are numerous and various. From an early period every fairy annalist concurred in giving to the king and queen of the fairies the name of Oberon and Titania. Titania, though not under this name, figures in the tale of Thomas Lermont, commonly called Thomas the Rhymer, one of the earliest traditions relative to the fairy tribe. Thomas was a distinguished poet and prophet, who lived near Melrose, and was proprietor of Ercildoune. The year of his birth is uncertain, but he was an old man when Edward I. was carrying on war in Scotland. His predictions have long excited interest in his native country. The following adventure, handed down in the words of an ancient ballad, befel this individual on the Eildon hills, in Roxburghshire:—

> True Thomas lay on Huntly bank,
>   A ferlie spied he with his e'e ;
> For there he saw a ladye bright
>   Come riding down by Eildon tree.
>
> Her shirt was o' the grass-green silk,
>   Her mantle o' the velvet fyne ;
> At ilka telt o' her horse's mane
>   Hung fifty siller bells and nine.

The saddle of this visionary beauty's steed was of ivory, inlaid with gold. She had a quiver of arrows at her back, with a bow in one hand, and the other led three beautiful hounds in a leash.

> True Thomas he pull'd off his cap,
>   And louted low down to his knee ;
> " All hail ! thou mighty queen of heaven,
>   For thy peer on earth I ne'er did see ! "
>
> " O no ! O no ! Thomas," she said,
>   " That name does not belang to me ;
> I am but the queen of fair Elfland,
>   That am hither come to visit thee."

By some spell this fairy queen made Thomas her slave. She became changed into a hideous hag, yet he was compelled to follow her. They entered a cavern, and after wading through pools of blood, in pitchy darkness for three days, they reached a beautiful orchard, where the lady resumed her former dignity and stateliness. She took him to a gorgeous castle, where he joined with lords, and knights, and ladies in dancing to the most exquisite music. At the end of what he thought a short time, the queen told him that he had been seven years in the castle, and that he might return home. On parting, she gifted him " with a tongue that could never lie ". There are numberless such fairy legends, but one is enough for a specimen. Some of the poor creatures arraigned in Scotland for witchcraft admitted having had correspondence with the fairies. The trials of Bessie Dunlop in 1576, and of Alison Pearson in 1588, illustrate this statement. Bessie Dunlop avowed that the ghost of one Thomas Reid appeared to her—a soldier slain at Pinkie in 1547—that he took her to fairyland, and introduced her to the queen. Alison Pearson also admitted her familiarity with the fairies, from whom she had received herbs for the cure of diseases. It is remarkable that Patrick Adamson, an able scholar and divine, who was created Archbishop of St. Andrews by James VI., actually took the medicines prescribed by this poor woman, in the hope that they would transfer an illness with which he was seized to the body of one of his horses. , These poor women were both convicted, and both were put to death at the stake. No doubt there are some in the Highlands and Islands who still believe in the existence of the fairy race. The " sithiche," or fairy, is the most active sprite in Highland mythology. It is a dexterous child-stealer, and must be carefully guarded against. At birth many covert and cunning ceremonies are still used to baffle the fairy's power, otherwise the new-born child would be taken off to fairyland, and a withered, little, living skeleton of a child laid in its stead. If offended, they are wantonly mischievous, and hurt severely, and perhaps kill with their arrows, such as annoy them. These arrows are of stone, like a yellow flint, and shaped like a barbed arrow-head. They are called "saighdean sithe," or fairy arrows. These arrow-heads must have been extensively used in their warfare by the aboriginal people of the Isles (and not, of course, by the fairies), as they are still picked up here and there in the fields, and are all much of the same size and shape. In Skye, and in the Hebrides in general, the fairies dwelt in green knolls or hillocks, called "sitheanan," and there is hardly a parish or district which has not its "sithean," or fairy-hill. I knew an old man in Skye who died about thirty years ago, at the age of about 100, whose name was Farquhar Beaton. He so firmly believed in fairies and other superstitions that in his "grace before meat" he prayed thus :—

O Thi bheannuichte, cum ruinn, agus cuidich leinn, agus na tuiteadh do ghras oirn mar an t-uisge air druim a' gheoidh. An uair a bhios fear 'na eigin air gob rutha, cuidich fein leis; agus bi mu'n cuairt duinn air tir, agus maille ruinn. Gleidh an t-aosda agus an t-oga, ar mnathan agus ar paisdean, ar spreidh agus ar feudal, o chumhachd agus o cheannas nan sithichean, agus o mhi-run gach droch-shula. Bitheadh slighe reidh romhainn, agus crioch shona aig ar turas.

Which may be translated thus :—

O Blessed One, provide for us and help us, and let not thy grace fall on us like the rain-drops on the back of a goose. When a man is in danger on the point of a promontory at sea, do thou succour him; and be about us and with us on dry land. Preserve the aged and the young, our wives and our children, our sheep and our cattle, from the power and dominion of the fairies, and from the malicious effects of every evil eye. Let a straight path be before us, and a happy end to our journey.

Many throughout the Highlands and Islands entertained

the same firm belief in the existence of fairies as poor old Farquhar Beaton did. They were generally deemed harmless sprites—"Daoine-sithe,"—beings that loved kindness and peace, yet they had their differences and quarrels; and desperate were their disputes when they took place. Old Farquhar spoke of many occasions when the fairy fights became fast and furious. The Macleods of Dunvegan, and the Macdonalds (commonly called the Lords of the Isles) at Duntulm, had their particular pipers, and their pipe-music colleges. The Macleods had the distinguished race of MacCrimmons for centuries, as family pipers, and they had their college at Boreraig, a tenement near Dunvegan, which they held free. In the same way, the Macdonalds had the famed MacArthurs as pipers, with the free possession of Peingowen for their college. A continued rivalry existed between the MacCrimmons and MacArthurs for supremacy in the musical art, and both had their particular fairy friends, who were said to supply them with reeds, and even, at times, with sets of bagpipes. As the famed Muses of Parnassus inspired their favourite bards with poetic powers, so the fairies conferred the requisite power on these family pipers to progress in the proficiency of their art. But at times, so keen were these gay coadjutors for the success of their particular musical protegès, that they disputed, and actually fought for the victory, thereby causing their "sian" dwellings to ring with the din of the conflict. Old Farquhar, when questioned as to his belief in these things, would raise his hands, and say, " Mo dha shuil fein a chunnaic iad ; mo dha chluas fein a chual iad." (My own two eyes beheld them ; my two ears heard them.) Farquhar was a thin, spare, hard-featured, little man, who prided himself on his ancestry, as a race distinguished for their knowledge of medicinal herbs. He could trace his genealogy from son to

sire, back to ten or twelve generations, as many others in
Skye could do in regard to themselves. Poor Farquhar had
a superstitious dislike to bacon or pork. For many years
before his death he had dinner at the Manse every Sabbath
by the minister's special request, when he invariably said the
above grace before commencing his meal. It frequently
happened that the servants' dinner consisted of pork or bacon,
the look of which Farquhar could not bear, and yet he often
dined on it. The servants, knowing his prejudices, had
beforehand prepared a quantity of the lean parts of the meat
for the old man, which they passed of as mutton, and which
he never suspected. While partaking of it, however, he
frequently said, to the nc small amusement and tittering of
the domestics—"Bu tu fein an fheoil mhaith, cheart, agus
cha b'i a' mhuc ghrannda, shalach"; (Thou art the good,
right meat, and not the filthy, unclean pig).

The fairies were said to be very fierce and vindictive when
altercations and differences took place among themselves,
and particularly so, when enemies injured or assailed those
with whom they were on friendly terms. The Jameses, who
were jolly monarchs, were in general most auspicious parti-
sans of these fantastic tribes; at least they considered those
royal personages as such. Perthshire was of old a noted
district for the intrigues of the fairies. The Clan Donnach-
aidh, or Robertson of Struan, were not generally favourites
with them. During the minority of James V., this powerful
clan committed bloody outrages over the district of Athole,
at which the fairies were so enraged that they contrived
means whereby the enemy waylaid the laird of Struan, while
visiting his uncle, and basely assassinated him in the presence
of his relative.*

In ancient times, the residence of the Athole family was

* Vide Buch. Lib. xiii.

B

a lofty, turreted mansion, possessing an air of grandeur characteristic of feudal times. It is said that it was within this lordly mansion that the cruel assassin of our first James meditated his bloody purpose. If credit can be given to Lindsay, the historian, it was here also, about a century afterwards, that an Earl of Athole entertained, in the most sumptuous manner, King James V. On that occasion, his Majesty entered the district of Athole with a numerous retinue, to hunt the deer of the Grampian hills. A banquet of extraordinary magnificence and splendour was furnished for the Scottish Monarch. A separate banquetting-hall was prepared, at a vast expense, for the entertainment of his Majesty and his retainers. Lindsay says, " That there was no want of meates, drinkes, and delicacies, that were to be gotten at that time in Scotland, either in brugh or land. So that he (the King) wanted none of his orders mare than he had been at home in his own palace. The King remained in this wilderness (i.e., Athole) at the hunting the space of three days and three nights, as I have shewn. I heard men say it cost the Earl of Athole every day in expenses a thousand pounds." No sooner had the royal visitor taken his departure than Athole, instigated, as was said, by the fairies, caused his Highlandmen to set fire to the temporary palace and huts which had been reared for the occasion, " that the King and the ambassadors might see them on fire ". Then the ambassador said to the King, " I marvel, Sir, that you should thole your fair palace to be burnt, that your grace has been so well lodged in ". Then the King answered,—" It is the use of our Highlandmen, though they be never so well lodged, to burn the lodgings when they depart."

"It would seem," says Lindsay, " the next visit the King paid to his Highlandmen, was not marked with so much merriment and banquetting as the former, for when the King

**passed** into the isles, and there held justice courts, and punished both thief and traitor, according to their demerits, syne brought many of the great men of the isles captive with him; such as Mudyart, Maconnel, Macloyd, Mackay, Macloyd of the Lewis, MacNeil, Maclane, Macintosh, John Mudyard, Mackenzie, with many others that I cannot rehearse at this time. Some of them he put in ward, and some bade in court, and some he took pledges for good rule in time coming. So he brought the isles, both north and south, in good rule and peace."

It was believed by the natives in these times, that the King had acquired power over these chieftains through the influence of the fairies, or some other evil spirits that had not been on friendly terms with the natives of the Isles, on account of some injuries received at their hands. Superstition in those days was at no loss to find a cause for every revolution and change.

Speaking of the fairies in olden times, they seem to have exercised their various pranks in different localities, still pointed out in the shires of Fife and Forfar, as well as in the counties around. The old Castle of Glammis, a venerable and majestic pile of building, has several fairy legends connected with it. In an underground part of this old edifice, there was a secret room, which was only known to two, or at most three individuals, at the same time, and these were bound not to reveal it, but to their successors in the secret. It is said to have been haunted, and at times taken possession of by ghosts and fairies. It has frequently been the object of search with the inquisitive, but the search has been in vain. Tradition gives one account, that Malcolm II. was murdered in this room in 1034, and that the murderers lost their way in the darkness of the night, and by the breaking of the ice were drowned in the loch of Forfar. Fordun gives a different account, and states that the King was mortally wounded in a skirmish near the Castle, and that an obelisk or large stone of rude design was erected to commemorate the murder, and not to represent the King's gravestone, as he was buried at Iona.

Near the summit of Carmylie hill is a large burrow or tumulus, which was believed at one time by the natives to be a favourite haunt of the fairies, where, with much splendour, they held their nightly revels. It still bears the name of "Fairy-folk hillock".

In the parish of Lunan, in Forfarshire, there is an immense variety of "knaps" or round hillocks, in different places. Very probably the knaps had been used as beacons in ancient times, to give notice of alarm on the approach of an enemy, by means of fires lighted upon them. It is, however, the case, that various fairy superstitions were connected with these "sians" or tumuli, of which mention is made to this day. One ancient practice existed, that the relatives of the dead, the day after the funeral, carried the chaff and bed-straw on which the body had lain to the knap nearest to the house, and there consumed them by fire. This superstition was prevalent in several parts of Scotland.

WITCHCRAFT.—This superstition took its rise in the East, and at an early period of the world's history. It was regarded as the power of magical incantation through the agency of evil spirits. From an early era, it was pursued as a trade by crafty wretches, who played upon the weakness of their fellow-creatures. Laws were passed against it. Many wretches were tortured in order to confess to it; and, to avoid these preliminary horrors, hundreds confessed all that they were accused of, and were forthwith led to execution. It has been calculated that, from the date of Pope Innocent's bull in 1484 to the final extinction of these persecutions, no fewer than 100,000 were put to death in Germany alone.

Witchcraft was first denounced in England in 1541, in the reign of Henry VIII.   Previous to that time, however, many witch trials had taken place, and severe punishments were inflicted.   We are all familiar with the fearful account of the witches near Forres, in the tragedy of Macbeth.   Queen Elizabeth, in 1562, directed a statute exclusively against witchcraft.   Many sad incidents are on record of the effects of this statute.*

The mind of King James VI. was deeply impressed with the flagrant nature of the crime of witchcraft.   Soon after his arrival from Denmark in 1590, to conduct his bride home, the Princess Anne, a tremendous witch conspiracy was formed against his Majesty's prosperity.   One Mrs. Agnes Sampson, commonly called " the wise wife of Keith" (a village of East Lothian), was the principal agent in this horrible work.   She was summoned before the King, and in the words of her trial it is recorded :—" The said Agnes Sampson was after brought again before the King's Majestie and his Council, and being examined of the meetings and detestable dealings of these witches, she confessed that upon the night of All Hallowe'en she was accompanied with a great many other witches, to the number of two hundred, and that all they together went to the sea, each one in a riddle or sieve, and went in the same, very substantially, with flaggons of wine, making merry and drinking by the way in the same riddles, or sieves, to the Kirk of North Berwick, in Lothian, and that after they had landed, took hands on the land, and danced this reil, or short dance, singing all with one voice—

<br>

> Cummer, goe ye before, Cummer goe ye ;
> Giff ye will not go before, Cummer, let me.

* For several of these in England and the South of Scotland, see *Celtic Magazine*, Vol. III., pp. 52-53.

One Geillis Duncan did go before them, playing this reil upon a small trump until they entered the Kirk of North Berwick.   These made the King in a wonderful admiration, and he sent for the said Geillis Duncan, who upon the like trump did play the said reill before the King's Majestie. Agnes Sampson declared that one great object with Satan and his agents was to destroy the King by raising a storm at sea when James came across from Denmark," and that "the witches demanded of the Divell, why he beare sic hatred to the King? who answered, by reason the King is the greatest enemie hee hath in the world."   Such an eulogy, from such a quarter, could not but pamper the conceit of the easily flattered Scottish monarch !

But we had some cases in the north, which showed that witchcraft was not confined to the lower classes.   Catherine Ross, or Lady Fowlis, was indicted by the King's advocate for the practice of witchcraft.   She was anxious to make young Lady Fowlis possessor of the property of Fowlis, and to have her married to the Laird of Balnagown.   Before this could be effected, she had to cut off her sons in-law, Robert and Hector Munro, and the young wife of Balnagown.   She proceeded to her deadly work by consulting with witches, making effigies of her intended victims in clay, and shooting at them with arrows, shod with elf-arrowheads.

The nature of these effigies of clay may be explained.   Such as were intended to be doomed, or destroyed, were formed of clay into hideous figures, or rude statues larger than life-size.   These were called "cuirp-creadha," or bodies of clay.   Once formed, incantations and spells were uttered over them.   Pins, nails, and feathers were pierced into them, and fairy arrows darted against them, with fearful oaths and imprecations.   Such things Lady Fowlis resorted to for de-stroying her relatives ; but when all failed, this abandoned woman had recourse to the poisoning of ales and certain dishes, by which she put several persons to death, though not the intended victims.  By the confession of some of the assistant hags, the purposes of Lady Fowlis were disclosed ; she was brought to trial, but was acquitted by a local jury.

These disgraceful proceedings were not without parallel in other distinguished families of the day.  Euphemia Macalzean, daughter of an eminent judge, Lord Cliftonhall, was burned at the stake for witchcraft in 1591.  This abandoned woman was found guilty by a jury for murdering her own godfather, as also her husband's nephew, and others, for which she was " burnt in assis, quick to the death".

In the beginning of the reign of Charles II., Morayshire became the scene of a violent fit of the great moral frenzy, and some of the most remarkable trials in the course of Scottish witchcraft took place there.  The last justiciary trial for witchcraft in Scotland was that of Elspeth Rule, who was convicted in 1708, and banished.  The last regular execution for this crime took place in Dornoch in 1722, when an old woman was condemned to death by David Ross, Sheriff of Caithness.  It is difficult to compute the number of the victims of witchcraft in Scotland, but attentive inquirers make out that the black list would include upwards of four thousand persons !  And by what a fate did they perish ?  Cruelly tortured while living, and dismissed from life by a living death amidst the flames !  And for what ? For an impossible crime.  And who were the victims, and who were the executioners !  The victims in most cases, were the aged, the weak, the deformed, the lame, and the blind—those, indeed, whom years and infirmities had doomed to poverty and wretchedness ; yes, exactly that class of miserable beings for whom Acts of Parliament have now made comfortable provision—those unfortunate creatures for whose benefit our more enlightened rulers now provide houses of refuge, erect poorhouses like palaces, build large asylums, and endow charitable institutions of every kind. But who were the executioners? The wisest, the greatest, and the most learned of their time—men distinguished above their fellows for knowledge and intelligence—ministers of religion and of the law, kings, princes, and nobles.

It is rather remarkable that, as late as January, 1871, a trial in regard to witchcraft took place in Newtonwards Quarter Sessions, in County Down. Hugh Kennedy sued his brother John for payment of a sum alleged to be due to him for wages and other services. He stated that his brother's house and land were frequented by witches, and that he had been employed to banish them. The witches did not belong to the "good people," and were maliciously inclined towards his brother—his land got into a bad condition, and his cows into a state of settled melancholy. There was a certain charm of great repute in the neighbourhood for putting to flight these unwelcome visitors; but it was only useful when properly applied and performed, and no other person but plaintiff could be got to undertake the task. The method pursued was thus :—The plaintiff locked himself in the house alone; he stopped up the keyholes, closed up the windows, stuffed up the chimney, and, in fact, left no mode of egress to the unfortunate witches whom he was to summons into his presence. He then lit a fire and put a pot of milk on it, and into the pot he put three rows of pins and needles, which had never been sullied or contaminated by use. These he boiled together for half-an-hour, during which time the witches were supposed to be suffering the most excruciating tortures, and had at last to take to flight. They had never been seen or heard of since. The cows resumed their former healthy condition, and the land its wonted fertility. The case being of a rather "complicated" nature, it was left to arbitration. Subsequently, it was announced in court, that the sum of 10s had been awarded to the plaintiff.

SECOND-SIGHT.—This is the faculty of seeing otherwise invisible objects. It is neither voluntary nor constant, and is considered rather annoying than agreeable to the possessors of it, who are chiefly found among the Highlands and Islands of Scotland, the Isle of Man and Ireland. The gift was possessed by individuals of both sexes, and its fits came on within doors and without, sitting and standing, at night and by day, and at whatever employment the votary might chance to be engaged. The visions were usually about funerals, shrouds, the appearance of friends who were at the time in distant countries, the arrival of strangers, falls from horses, the upsetting of vehicles, bridal ceremonies, funeral processions, corpses, swamping of boats, drowning at sea, dropping suddenly dead, and numberless other subjects. Very astonishing cases might be mentioned wherein it would appear impossible that either fraud or deception could exist. Martin, in his book on the Western Isles, alludes to many who were undoubtedly, in his belief, "Taibhsears," or Seers; and even to this day this faculty is believed by many to exist. Dr. Beattie ascribes it to the influence of physical causes on superstitious and unenlightened minds, such as the effects which wild scenery, interspersed with valleys, mountains, and lakes, have upon the imagination of the natives. Others maintain that it arose from optical illusions, and others from ignorance, the great mother of all superstitions. It is remarkable when Dr. Samuel Johnson visited Skye in 1773, and had heard much about the second-sight, that he gave credit to it, and expressed his surprise that it was disbelieved by the clergy, while many others were of a different opinion. If space permitted, many wonderful cases of second-sight might be given, but a few must suffice. It is traditionally stated that the execution of the unfortunate Queen Mary had been foreseen by many Highland seers, and had been previously described by them by extraordinary minuteness. King James alludes to it in his " Demonology"; and it was brought as a charge against various Shetland witches in that monarch's reign. Mackenzie of Tarbat, afterwards Earl of Cromartie, a talented statesman in the reign of Charles II., wrote some account of this strange faculty for the use of the celebrated Boyle. He gives one instance, as follows :—One day as he was riding in a field among his tenants, who were manuring barley, a stranger came up to the party and observed that they need not be so busy about their crop, as he saw the Englishmen's horses tethered among them already. The event proved as the man had foretold, for the horses of Cromwell's army in 1650 ate up the whole field. A few years after this incident, before Argyll went on his fatal journey to congratulate King Charles on his restoration, he was playing at bowls with some gentlemen near his castle at Inverary, when one of them grew pale and fainted as the Marquis stooped for his bowl. On recovering, he cried, " Bless me, what do I see? my lord with his head off, and all his shoulders full of blood". The late General Stewart of Garth, in his "Sketches of the Highlanders," relates a very remarkable instance of second-sight which happened in his own family :—" Late on an autumnal evening in the year 1773, the son of a neighbouring gentleman came to my father's house. He and my mother were from home, but several friends were in the house. The young gentleman spoke little, and seemed absorbed in deep thought. Soon after he arrived, he inquired for a boy of the family, then three years of age. When shown into the nursery, the nurse was trying on a pair of new shoes, and complained that they did not fit the child. ' They will fit him before he will have occasion for them,' said the young gentleman. This called forth the chidings of the nurse for predicting evil to the child, who was stout and healthy. When he returned to the party he had left in the sitting-room, who had heard of his observation on the shoes, they cautioned him to take care that the nurse did not derange his new talent of the second sight, with some ironical congratulations on his pretended acquirement. This brought on an explanation, when he told them that as he had approached the end of a wooden bridge near the house, he was astonished to see a crowd of people passing the bridge. Coming nearer, he observed a person carrying a small coffin, followed by about twenty gentlemen, all of his acquaintance, his own father and mine being of the number, with a concourse of the country people. He did not attempt to join, but saw them turn off to the right, in the direction of the churchyard, which they entered. He then proceeded on his intended visit, much impressed with what he had seen, with a feeling of awe, and believing it to have been a representation of the death and funeral of a child of the family. The whole received perfect confirmation in his mind, by the sudden death of the boy the following night, and the consequent funeral, which was exactly as he had seen. This gentleman was not a professed seer. This was his first and his last vision, and, as he told me," says General Stewart, " it was sufficient."

A very remarkable instance of supernatural vision happened a few years ago, in a landed proprietor's house in Skye. On a certain evening, probably that of New Year's Day, a large party of neighbouring ladies and gentlemen, with the youngsters of their families, had been invited to enjoy certain harmless festivities at this proprietor's house, the lady of which had been absent at the time in the south, but her sons and daughters were at home to entertain the happy guests. After dinner the junior members of the party retired to the drawing-room to amuse themselves. A quadrille was set agoing, but before it had commenced, the figure of a lady glided along the side wall of the room, from end to end, and was seen by several of those opposite to it. " My mother ! my mother !" screamed one of the young ladies of the family, and fainted. The vision put a sudden termination to the hilarities of the evening ; but the most surprising fact was, that at the very time the vision appeared, the lady of the house had died in a city in the south.

Besides the many instances of second-sight given by Martin, Theophilus Insulanus, and several others, a great additional variety might be stated of rather remarkable cases. In the village of Earlish, parish of Snizort, in Skye, about fifty years ago, a cottar's wife was delivered of a nice baby. Soon after the birth, the happy mother was visited by the wives of her neighbours, who came, according to the custom of the place on such occasions, each with a gift of fowls, eggs, and such like. The baby was admired as a nice infant, and the usual hopes were expressed that it might be long spared to the parents. One female in a corner of the apartment whispered in her neighbour's ear, that she was afraid the infant would not be long spared, and that it would some day be the cause of excessive grief to the poor mother. On being questioned for the reason of such a statement, she said that she had a vision of the child all mangled, torn up, and bleeding. Her neighbour upbraided her for expressing a thing so ridiculous in itself, and so very improbable. In the course of a month or two, when the infant had progressed in health and strength to the desire of his parent's heart, he was laid to sleep in the cradle, and the mother, being alone at the time, embraced the opportunity of going to the well for a pitcher of water. After having talked for a few minutes with a neighbour who had met her at the well, she returned to her house, when, to her unspeakable horror, she found her baby on the floor dead, mangled, torn to pieces, with the arms and face eaten away. During the distracted mother's absence, a large brute of a pig had been roaming about. It entered the deserted apartment, seized upon the innocent sleeping babe, and partially devoured it.

About sixty years ago, one of the annual fairs was to be held at Portree, the Capital of Skye, to which the natives were in the habit of resorting in hundreds from all quarters of the Island. In the East-side district of Kilmuir, about eighteen miles north of Portree, there lived at that time a female advanced in years, who was reported to be possessed of the faculty of second-sight. Some time previous to the date of the market, this woman was day after day sitting, sighing, and lamenting the catastrophe, which she said was sure to take place, as she had seen a boat sinking in a storm, and so many people drowned. Few, however, paid any attention to the cause of her grief at the time, but there was reason afterwards to do so. A large boat left Portree on the market-day evening for the East-side, which was literally crammed with people of all ages, anxious to get home. A storm got up, and all were consigned to a watery grave.

Here is another remarkable instance. A worthy parish minister in Skye, about seventy years ago, went to visit a brother of his, a Captain Macleod, who had been ailing, and lived near Portree. Captain Macleod had a numerous family of sons and daughters. In the evening, the minister mounted his horse to return home, a distance of about nine miles. The weather became so boisterous and stormy, that the good old gentleman deemed it prudent to pass the night at Scorribreck, where Widow Nicolson and her family resided. She was a sister of the late Adjutant-General Sir John Macdonald. Mrs. Nicolson welcomed her reverend guest, and was delighted at his unexpected appearance. At that remote period most of the large farmers' dwellings in Skye, were comfortable thatched houses, with trap-stairs to the upper flats, where they deposited all kinds of lumber. In a certain corner up-stairs in this domicile, the parish mort-cloth was kept for safety, as the burying-place was near by. Mrs. Nicolson ascended the stairs on some business in the dark, and left the reverend gentleman with her family for a few minutes in the parlour. Immediately thereafter a scream was heard, instantly followed by the noise of a fall on the upper floor. Two or three rushed up with a light, and found Mrs. Nicolson in a fainting fit, quite insensible. On her recovering, and at a subsequent hour of the evening, she reluctantly told her reverend friend that she beheld a very brilliant light on the mort-cloth, which was spread on a table, and in the middle of the light she saw the distinct image of his niece's face, a daughter of the said Captain Macleod. The circumstance, no doubt, created some concern in the minds of the family circle, but ere bed-time, the conversation turned on something else. Shortly thereafter, however, the young lady alluded to, took ill, and died, and her bier was the first to require the use of the mort-cloth in question after that eventful evening.

Another instance equally marvellous took place in the northern district of Skye, at a considerably later date than that of the event just recorded. The parish clergyman on his rounds, visited the miller's house, and met the miller's wife evidently in a very excited state, standing on the kitchen floor. In that part of the Island great quantities of timber were frequently found on the sea-shore, drifted thither from wrecked vessels. On this occasion the miller's kitchen was benched all round with batons and planks of timber, in order to be seasoned by the heat of the fire, which is placed in these dwellings in the middle of the floor. . The clergyman had scarcely time to speak, when the goodwife, a very respectable woman, told him that she was always glad to see him, but particularly so on this occasion. She explained that Christy Macleod, a female of known repute as a seer, had just been sitting on that plank, warming herself by the fire, when she suddenly fainted and fell on the floor. She further stated that she carried Christy ben the house, and laid her on a bed until she would recover. "But," said the matron to the minister, "you must go to see Christy, and insist upon her telling what she saw, as I am in terror that she had an unlucky sight of some of my own children." The minister very reluctantly complied, and, on entering the apartment, found Christy so far recovered as to bear being questioned. He asked the cause of her ailment, and, in short, put the query whether she had seen anything? She refused to reply, except by the uttering of some evasive answers. He then told her to tell at once what she had seen, as otherwise he would not leave her until she did. Eventually she expressed herself in timid, tremulous terms, and said, that while seated on the wooden bench by the fire, she happened to cast her eyes upon a plank on the opposite side, and beheld stretched on it the mangled, bleeding body of a lad, Macdonald, then alive and well. Having told this, she solicited the minister not to divulge it. On his leaving the seer, he was instantly pounced upon by the landlady, and asked, in breathless anxiety, "What did she see? What or whom did she see?" His reverence had no alternative but to tell the good matron, for the comfort of herself and her domestic circle, what the dreaded woman had revealed. All parties were then contented, and the affair looked on as a mere revery. Six weeks or so thereafter, there was a marriage in the upper district of the parish, to which the young man, Macdonald, was invited, and went. On returning home alone about midnight by a hilly pathway, in the extreme darkness, he lost his way, fell over a precipice about a thousand feet high, and was dashed to pieces in the clefts of the debris below. He was eventually missed at home. Messengers were sent in quest of him, hither and thither, and when no tidings could be found concerning him, the population of the district went forth in hundreds on the search. After a day or two's minute ransacking of every hill and dale, lake and river, the mangled corpse was discovered by a boy, jammed hard and fast in a crevice at the base of the huge precipice already named. The crowd assembled around the shattered remains, and a cry was uttered as to what was best to be done? The torn body could hardly be handled, and a proposal was immediately agreed to, that four men should run to the miller's house for a door or plank, to convey the remains to the father's home. This was done —the men rushed forward to the miller's, and snatched away the identical plank on which the woman, Macleod, had seen the vision already related.

Many similar instances of second-sight in the Western Isles are alleged to have existed, which as yet have not been recorded.

It is stated in the Statistical Account of Iona, that St. Columba was the first on record who had the faculty of second-sight. He is said to have told the victory of Aidan over the Picts and Saxons, on the very instant it happened. The same authority states, that when St. Columba first attempted to build on Iona, the walls, by the operation of

some evil spirit, fell down as fast as they were erected.
Columba received some supernatural information that they
would never stand unless a human victim was buried alive.
According to one account, the lot fell on Oran, the companion
of the Saint, as the victim that was demanded for the success
of the undertaking.   Others pretend that Oran voluntarily
devoted himself, and was interred accordingly.   At the end
of three days, Columba had the curiosity to take a farewell
look at his old friend, and caused the earth to be removed
accordingly.   Oran raised his swimming eyes, and said,
"There is no wonder in death, and hell is not as it is
reported".   The Saint was so shocked at this monstrous
impiety, that he instantly ordered the earth to be flung in
again, uttering the words, " Uir ! Uir ! air beul Orain ! mu'n
labhair e tuilleadh comhraidh !"—that is, Earth ! Earth ! on
the mouth of Oran, that he may blab no more !   This passed
into a proverb, and is in use in the Highlands at the present
day.   It is not improbable that the story was invented by
some of Columba's Druidical enemies to expose him and his
Christian doctrines to ridicule.

SMALLER SUPERSTITIONS.—Somewhat resembling this alleged faculty, yet different from it, are certain prognosti-
cations of death, which are said to be seen in the shape of
blue, quivering lights, resembling the feeble flame of a taper.
These have been observed moving along in the course which
some funeral procession would soon take, or perhaps twink-
ling in or about the bed on which some individual was soon
to die.   Many intelligent people firmly believe in the
existence of these lights.

Some years ago, if not even still, many in the Western
Isles believed in the existence of the " Gruagach," a female
spectre of the class of Brownies to which the Highland

dairymaids made frequent libations of milk. The Gruagach is said to have been an innocent, supernatural visitor, who frisked and gambolled about the cattle-pens and folds. She was armed only with a pliable reed, with which she switched all who annoyed her by uttering obscene language, or would neglect to leave for her a share of the dairy produce. Even so late as 1770, the dairymaids who attended a herd of cattle in the Island of Trodda, at the north end of Skye, were in the habit of pouring daily a quantity of milk on a hollow stone for the Gruagach. Should they neglect to do so, they made sure of feeling the effects of her wand next day. The Rev. Dr. Macqueen, then minister of Kilmuir, of whom Dr. Johnson spoke so highly, and who is buried within a few yards of Flora Macdonald's grave, went purposely to Trodda to check this gross superstition. He might then have succeeded for a time, but it is known that many believed in the existence of the Gruagach long after that worthy clergyman had been gathered to his fathers. Besides the votaries of this ridiculous superstition, there are others who confidently believe in the existence of an evil eye, by which cattle and all kinds of property are said to suffer injury. The glance of an evil eye is, therefore, very much dreaded. It deprives cows of their milk, and milk of its nutritive qualities, and renders it unfit for the various preparations made from it. This superstition can certainly lay claim to great antiquity. Virgil, Ossian, and other writers, seem to have dreaded the effects of it, at least they allude to its existence. Virgil says (Eclog. III., 103)—

> Nescio quis teneros oculus mihi fascinat agnos.
> (I know not what malignant eye bewitches my tender lambs).

But equally superstitious are the means resorted to for the cure of these sad afflictions, such as the use of certain charms, the repetition of strange rhymes, putting living trout in a portion of the injured milk, and many other such ridiculous appliances.

There is an endless variety of superstitions in regard to things which are unlucky or unfortunate to be done. It is unfortunate if a stranger counts the number of your sheep, cattle, or children. It is quite common if one asks, "How many children have you?" to add the words, "Bless them" to the question. It is unlucky for an odd number to sit at a table, such as 7, 9, 11; and 13 in particular is so unfortunate that unless rectified, one of the party is sure to die that year. It is unlucky if a stranger walks across a parcel of fishing-rods on the sea beach, over ropes, oars, or sailing gear, when a boat is about to go to sea. Means are used for getting the stranger to retrace his steps. It is unlucky to drink the health of a company, or to serve them round a table except from left to right, as the sun goes in the firmament, or the hands on the dial-plate of a watch. It is unlucky, in setting off, to row in a boat, or to commence a procession at a marriage or funeral, but to the right. It is unlucky to hear the cuckoo, or see a foal or snail before breakfast. As to this there is a Gaelic rhyme as follows, viz. :—

> Chunnaic mi an searrachan 'sa chulaobh rium,
> Chunnaic mi an t-seilcheag air an lic luim ;
> Chual mi' a' chuag gun ghreim 'nam bhroinn,
> Is dh' aithnich mi fein nach rachadh a' bhliadhn' so leam.

These lines may be translated—

> With its back to me turn'd I beheld the young foal,
> And the snail on the bare flag in motion so slow ;
> Without tasting of food, lo ! the cuckoo I heard,
> Then judged that the year would not prosperously go.

It is unlucky to stand between an epileptic man and fire or

water.  In Shetland there was once an idea that it was un-lucky to save drowning men.  It is unlucky to throw out water after sunset, and before sunrise.  It is unlucky to have a grave open upon Sunday, as another will be dug during the week for some of the family.  If a corpse does not stiffen after death, there will be another death in the family before the end of that year.  Fires and candles afford presages of death.  Long hollow coals spirted from the fire are coffins. Winding-sheets are indicated when the tallow of the candle curls away from the flame.  The howling of a dog at night, and the resting of a crow or magpie on the house-top, are warnings of death.  It is unlucky to weigh infants ; they are sure to die.  Cats sleeping near infants suck their breath and kill them.  When children begin to walk they must go up-stairs before they go down-stairs, otherwise they will not thrive in the world, and if there is no stair they should climb a chair.  A mother after the birth of a child must not go outside beyond her house door until she goes to be kirked. If you rock an empty cradle you will soon rock a new baby in it.  It is quite curious to see the face of alarm with which a poor woman, with her tenth baby in her arms, will dash across the room to prevent " the baby but one " from the dangerous amusement of rocking the empty cradle.  It is unlucky that a stray swarm of bees should settle on your premises unclaimed by their owner.  It is customary in many parts of England when a death takes place to go and tell the bees of it, to ask them to the funeral, and to fix a piece of crape upon their hives !  It is unlucky to catch a sight of the new moon through a window.  It is a token of fine weather to see the old moon in the arms of the new ; and so is the turning up of the horns of the new moon, as they retain the water which would fall to the earth if the horns were turned down.  It is unlucky to enter a house,

which you are to occupy, by the back door. If, when fishing
you count what you have taken, you will catch no more. If
you break your bones by accident, it is unlucky and useless
to employ a physician or surgeon to bind them, as it is
believed that, however skilful these may be in curing all
other maladies, they know nothing whatever about the setting
of broken bones.

Many other remarkable cures are resorted to, such as
healing sore eyes by putting gold rings in the ears, by
rubbing them with jewels of pure gold, and by repeating
certain rhymes. Warts are removed by washing them in
rain-water or swine's blood. Serpents' heads are preserved
for years to heal their own sting wounds. If a man, cow, or
any animal be stung by a serpent, let the dried serpent's head
be cast into water, let the wound be washed in it, and it soon
heals. Fried mice are a specific for small-pox. Whooping-
cough is cured by whatever is recommended by a person
riding a piebald horse. A spider put into a goose-quill, well
sealed, and put round a child's neck, will cure it of the
thrush. In the Island of Soa, near Skye, it was customary
when the head of the family died to have a large lock of
hair cut off his head and nailed fast to the door-lintel to keep
off the fairies. Sailors are sometimes very superstitious.
They greatly dread the stormy petrel, or Mother Carey's
chickens, as they flutter at night around their masts and
yards. These birds are regarded as objects of superstitious
fear, believing that they are possessed of supernatural agency
in creating danger for the poor, hard-toiled mariner. At
one time, a horse-shoe nailed to the mast of the vessel was
great security against all evil agencies, such as witches, petrels,
fairies, and evil eyes. To recapitulate all such superstitious
frets would be an endless task. There are many similar
fanciful notions in regard to births, baptisms, marriages, and

deaths, but it is impossible to enlarge much upon them. It was once prevalent when a child was baptised, that the infant was neither washed nor bathed that night, for fear of washing off the baptismal water before it had slept under it. Frequently too, the water used in baptism was bottled up as an effectual recipe for various disorders. Parents took all possible care lest their female infants should be baptised with the same water used for male children, for if they should, the females would grow up with beards! A few years ago, I was baptising two or three children at the same time, in a village near by, when the first presented was a boy, and the next a girl. After the water had been sprinkled on the face of the boy, and when I was about to do the same to the girl, an old worthy granny present hastily snatched away the bowl containing the water, poured it out, and filled it afresh, muttering aloud, " Na leigeadh Ni Math gum biodh feusag air mo chaileig" (Goodness forbid that my lassie should have a beard).

It is reckoned very unlucky in some parts of the country to have a child left unbaptised beyond the year in which it was born. For example, should a child come into the world on the 30th December, 1877, the parents would feel very uncomfortable, and consider it a neglect of duty, if they did not get the infant baptised either on that or next day.

Even in England peculiar frets are still observed in regard to infants. In a late number of an English paper, the following paragraph appeared :—" A certain act of barbarity and superstition is practised in many parts of the country. Children who are sickly are taken to a woman for the purpose of being cut for a supposed disease, called the Spinnage. The infants are, on a Monday morning, taken to this woman, who, for threepence, with a pair of scissors, cuts through the lobe of the right ear, then makes a cross with the blood

upon the forehead and breast of the child.   On the following
Monday the same barbarous ceremony is performed upon
the left ear, and on the succeeding Monday the right ear is
again doomed to undergo the same ceremony.   In some
cases, it is deemed necessary to perform this ridiculous
operation nine times.   It is not the lower classes alone who
are chargeable with this and similar follies.   Some of the
higher classes likewise observe them.   It is quite common
to make the children partake of a roasted mouse as a cure
for whooping-cough."

The cold-bath was so much esteemed by the Highlanders
in ancient times that, as soon as an infant was born, he was
plunged into a running stream, and then carefully wrapped
in a warm blanket.   Immediately thereafter, the little
creature was forced to swallow a large quantity of fresh
butter.   It was made into a ball of no ordinary size, and
was pressed down its little throat, in a manner sufficient to
create a fear of the poor child being suffocated.   Another
fret was observed, that immediately after a child was baptised,
he behoved to be secured from the power of the fairies, and
of all evil spirits.   For this purpose a basket was taken,
which was half filled with bread and cheese, wrapped up in
a clean linen cloth.   Over this parcel the child was laid as
if in a cradle.   The basket was then taken up by the oldest
female in the family circle at the time, carried three times
round the fire, and then suspended for a few seconds from
the crook that hung over the fire.   The child was then removed from its temporary berth, while the bread and cheese
were divided among the company present, as nourishment to
guarantee their health for another year.   There was still
another superstition, that soon after the birth of a child,
when all the duties necessary on such occasions had been
performed, it was customary to make a dish of " crowdie "

by mixing oaten meal and water together, of which each of the company required to take three horn-spoonfuls, for the protection of the infant. This superstition was, until of late, very prevalent in the Highlands of Perthshire. It was likewise the custom that the mother of the infant dare not perform any work, or engage herself in any of her domestic affairs, until she had been kirked. After she had performed this religious rite, and had dealt out a portion of bread and cheese to every one she met on her way home from the place of worship, she was invested with free liberty to attend to her ordinary household concerns. Until then, however, everything she did, and every object she handled, was reckoned unclean, and would not be meddled with by any in the family circle.

It was also alleged by carpenters that, while in bed at night, they heard their saws, hammers, and planes at work before being employed next day in making a coffin. Highlanders in particular speak confidently of the expected nature of the weather, from the figure, appearance, colour, coming, and stages of the moon. They avoid slaughtering sheep, pigs, and cattle in the wane of the moon, as the meat would shrink in cooking. In the same way they study to shear corn, to mow grass, to fell trees, and to cut peats and turf in the wane of the moon, as the best time for drying and seasoning these commodities.

There was a superstition in Ross-shire whereby it was believed that the soul did not finally and completely leave the body until the corpse had been laid in the grave. There was a similar superstition in Perthshire, whereby it was believed that at the moment of dissolution, whether by a natural death or by accident the soul or spirit was visibly seen leaving the body in the shape of a little creature like a bee. Witches frequently put themselves into the appearance of animals, such as a hare, but when arrows were pointed at them, barbed with silver, or muskets loaded with silver coins for shot, the semblance of the hare disappeared at once, and some shrivelled, decrepit hag of a witch wife stood before the shooter in full size !

The natives of Easter Ross, particularly the fishermen on the sea-coast from Tain to Cromarty Bay, are influenced to this day by remarkable superstitious frets which they observe on marriage occasions. It is the practice among them that couples, once the marriage festivities are past, must go to be kirked on the Sunday. This devout duty is easily performed when there is but one marriage in the place. But should there be two or three, as frequently occurs, in the same week, the kirking affair is entirely altered, and becomes a matter of no small difficulty and concern. Sabbath comes, and each marriage party, bridegroom and bride, with their attendants, prepare themselves for the parish church; duly arrive there in good time ; and perhaps desert their usual seats, through a desire to occupy those that happen to be nearest to the door. The sermon is impatiently listened to, when, without waiting perhaps for the benediction, the parties rush out, like so many bees from a hive, and run homewards as fast as their feet can carry them. Thus, one marriage party strives with another, in running the lucky race. Frequently, in their haste, the bridegroom outruns the bride and others of the party. All this arises from an old superstition, that the marriage party which first arrives at home from the kirking are sure to be prosperous and happy in after life, whereas those left behind, should it only be a distance of a few yards, run the risk of becoming the victims of misfortune and adversity.

The Highlanders, as well as many other ancient tribes, looked upon certain days as lucky or unlucky in themselves.

The 14th of May was considered an untoward day; so much so, that the day of the week on which the 14th day of May fell, was deemed unlucky during the whole of that year, and nothing of consequence was undertaken on that day. May and January were considered unfortunate months to marry in, as also the Friday of any week.

On the death of a Highlander, many silly superstitions were practised. In some districts it was believed that when death ensued, the spirit still kept close to the body, as if it were to guard it until after the burial, when dust was consigned to dust, and ashes to ashes. The relatives, friends, and neighbours of the deceased, deemed it their duty likewise to watch the corpse of the dead, both by night and by day. This was called the "late wake," at which the most absurd fooleries were practised, such as music, called the "coronach," dancing, leaping, riddles, games, singing of songs, and the most boisterous revelry. These manners and customs are now, however, almost extinct. There are many superstitious observances at certain seasons of the year, of which we must treat briefly.

I. "La Calluinn" and "Oidhche Challuinn" (New Year's Day and New-Year's Night). Besides the "first-footing," which is a common practice still, the Highlanders observed many in-door and out-door ceremonies. On New-Year's Eve, they surrounded each other's houses, carrying dried cow-hides, and beating them with sticks, thrashing the walls with clubs, all the time crying, shouting, and repeating rhymes. This is supposed to operate as a charm against fairies, demons, and spirits of every order. They provide themselves with the flap, or hanging part of the hide on the cow's neck, which they called "caisean-uchd," and which they singed in the fire and presented to the inmates of the family, one after another, to smell, as a charm against all injuries from fairies and spirits.  A specimen of the rhymes repeated, with loud chorus, is as follows :—

| | |
|---|---|
| Mor-phiseach air an tigh, | Great good luck to the house, |
| Piseach air an teaghlach, | Good luck to the family, |
| Piseach air gach cabar, | Good luck to every rafter of it, |
| Is air gach ni saoghalt' ann. | And to every wordly thing in it. |
| Piseach air eich a's crodh, | Good luck to horses and cattle, |
| Piseach air na caoraich, | Good luck to the sheep, |
| Piseach air na h-uile ni, | Good luck to every thing, |
| 'S piseach air ar maoin uil'. | And good luck to all your means. |
| Piseach air beann an tighe, | Luck to the good-wife, |
| Piseach air na paistean, | Good luck to the children, |
| Piseach air gach caraide, | Good luck to every friend, |
| Mor-phiseach agus slaint dhuibh. | Great fortune and health to all. |

II. "Di-domhnuich-caisg" (Easter Sunday).  This period is observed in the Highlands by preparing and eating certain kinds of pan-cakes made of eggs, milk, meal, or flour.  Together with this the young people provide themselves with large quantities of hard-boiled dyed eggs, which they roll about, and finally eat.  The English hot cross buns at Easter are only the cakes which the Saxons ate in honour of their goddess " Eastre," and from which the Christian clergy, who were unable to prevent people from eating them, sought to expel the Paganism by marking them with the cross.  Hence the hot cross buns.

III. "La Bealtuinn" (May-day, Whitsuntide).  The demonstrations of this day are now all but extinct.  The first of May was held as a great Druidical festival in honour of the mighty Asiatic god, Belus.  Fires were kindled on the mountain-tops, through which all the cattle of the country were driven to preserve them till the next May-day.  On this day all the hearth-fires were extinguished, in order to be kindled from this purifying flame.  Hence the word Bealtuinn is " Beil-teine," the fire of Belus.  So that " La Bealtuinn" (Whitsunday) is " the day of Belus' fire".  Of old in the Highlands the young people went to the moors on this day, made a circular table on the grass, cut a trench around it, kindled a huge fire, baked a large cake, which they cut into as many similiar pieces as there were persons present. They daubed one of the pieces with charcoal, and made it perfectly black.  Then they put all the bits of cake into a bonnet, from which all of them, blindfolded, drew a bit.

Whoever drew the black bit was the person who was doomed to be sacrificed to Baal ; and in order to avoid the execution of this doom, he was compelled to leap six times over the flames.  Even in Ayrshire, Baal's fire was kindled till about the year 1790.

HALLOWE'EN.—The only other season noted for superstitious observances is that of Hallowe'en.  Hallowe'en in Gaelic means "Samhuinn," that is "Samhtheine," the fire of peace.  It is a Druidical festival, at which the fire of peace was regularly kindled.  There is no night in the year which the popular imagination has stamped with a more peculiar character than Hallowe'en.  It was the night, above all others, when supernatural influences prevailed.  It was the night for the universal walking abroad of all sorts of spirits, fairies, and ghosts, all of whom had liberty on that night.  It was customary in many parts of Scotland to have hundreds of torches prepared in each district for weeks before Hallowe'en, so that, after sunset on that evening, every youth able to carry a blazing torch, or "samhnag," ran forth to surround the boundaries of their farms with these burning lights, and thereby protect all their possessions from the fairies.  Having thus secured themselves by these  fires of peace, all the households congregated to practice the various ceremonies and superstitious rites of that eventful evening.  As these are pretty fully alluded to in Burns' poem of " Hallowe'en," it is unnecessary to enlarge here.   There is still a remarkable uniformity in these fireside customs all over the kingdom. Nuts and apples are everywhere in requisition.   These the old matron of the house has generally in store beforehand for the youngsters' good luck on that night, or as the Ayrshire Bard has so naturally expressed it—

> The auld guidwife's weel hoordit nits
>   Are round and round divided,
> And mony lads' and lasses' fate
>   Are there that night decided.
> Some kindle couthie, side by side,
>   And burn thegither trimly ;
> Some start awa' wi' saucy pride,
>   And jump out-owre the chimley,
>     Fu' high that night.

The ceremonies of the evening were numerous—such as, ducking for apples in a tub of water, the pulling of kail stocks, the three dishes or "luggies," the wetting of the shirt sleeve, the sowing of hemp seed, pulling the stalks of corn, throwing the clue of blue yarn into the pit of the kiln, the white of eggs put into a glass of water, reading of fortunes in tea-cups ; these and many more were the superstitious ceremonies of Hallowe'en.

Perhaps there is no part of the Highlands of Scotland where the practice of using the flaming torches of Hallowe'en is so much observed, even still, as in the braes of Aberdeenshire.   Not later than last year, our Gracious Majesty, no doubt in order to preserve those relics of ancient times, caused these blazing torches to be kindled by the youth of the place, around Balmoral Castle.   The torches are considered by the natives to be the means of protecting, not only their farms and other possessions from the ravages of the fairies, but likewise mothers and newly-born infants.   While

the landed possessions were duly surrounded that evening by
the torch-bearers, the dwellings where children had been
born were encompassed with still greater care, for the safety
of the mothers and their young offspring, which the fairies
were on the watch to snatch away.   The torch-bearers used
great care in carrying their fire in the right-hand, and therewith running around their premises from right to left, thus
observing the " Deas-iuil," or the right hand direction.   The
" Tuath-iuil," being the left-hand, or wrong direction, would
render their precautions entirely abortive.   In this manner
they protected their properties, and prevented the fairy thieves
from snatching away the unbaptised infants from their mothers' bed, placing in their room their own ugly and deformed
children.   Martin, in his *History of the Western Isles*,
informs us, " That this was considered an effectual means to
preserve both the mother and infant from the power of evil
spirits, who are ready at such times to do mischief, and
sometimes carry away the infants, and return poor, meagre
skeletons ; and these infants have voracious appetites.   In
this case it was usual for those who believed that their
children were thus taken away, to dig a grave in the fields on
quarter-day, and there to lay the fairy-skeleton till next
morning, at which time the parents went to the place, where
they doubted not to find their own child instead of the
skeleton."   They had also, in other localties, recourse to
the barbarous charm of burning, with a live coal, the toes
of the suffering infant, the supposed changeling.   The Fairies
were not contented with abstracting handsome children—
beautiful maidens and wives sometimes disappeared.

" The Miller of Menstrie," in Clackmannan, who possessed
a charming spouse, had given offence to the fairy court, and
was, in consequence, deprived of his fair helpmate.   His dis-
tress was aggravated by hearing his wife singing in the air—

Oh ! Alva woods are bonnie,
Tillicoultry hills are fair ;
But when I think o' the bonnie braes o' Menstrie,
It mak's my heart aye sair.

After many attempts to procure her restoration, the miller chanced one day, in riddling some stuff at the mill-door, to use a posture of enchantment, when the spell was dissolved, and the matron fell into his arms. The wife of the Blacksmith of Tullibody was carried up the chimney, the fairies, as they bore her off, singing—

Deidle linkum doddie ;
We've gotten drucken Davie's wife,
The smith o' Tullibody.

"Those snatched to Fairyland," says Dr. Buchan,[*] "might be recovered within a year and a day, but the spell for the recovery was only potent when the fairies made, on Hallowe'en, their annual procession." Sir Walter Scott relates the following :—" The wife of a Lothian farmer had been watched by the fairies. During the year of probation, she had repeatedly appeared on Sundays in the midst of her children, combing their hair. On one of these occasions she was accosted by her husband, when she instructed him how to rescue her at the next Hallowe'en procession. The farmer conned his lesson carefully, and, on the appointed day, proceeded to a plot of furze to await the arrival of the procession. It came, but the ringing of the fairy bridles so confused him, that the train passed ere he could sufficiently recover himself to use the intended spell. The unearthly laugh of the abductors, and the passionate lamentations of his wife informed him that she was lost to him for ever."

[*] Dr. Buchan, Secretary of the Lancashire Insurance Company at Inverness, a gentleman rarely surpassed in his knowledge of Celtic Legendary Traditions and Folklore, and to whom the writer is much indebted for these remarks on Hallowe'en.

" A woman," says Dr. Buchan, " who had been conveyed to fairyland, was warned by one she had formerly known as a mortal, to avoid eating and drinking with her new friends for a certain period. She obeyed, and when the time expired, she found herself on earth restored to the society of mankind."

A matron on another occasion was carried to fairyland to nurse her new-born child, which had been previously abducted. She had not been long in her enchanted dwelling when she furtively anointed an eye with the contents of a boiling cauldron. She now discovered that what had previously seemed a gorgeous palace, was, in reality, a gloomy cavern. She was dismissed, but one of the wicked wights, when she demanded her child, spat in her eye, and extinguished its light for ever.

About the middle of last century, a clergyman at Kirkmichael, Perthshire, whose faith was more regulated by the scepticism of philosophy, than the credulity of superstition, would not be prevailed upon to yield his assent to the opinion of the times. At length, however, he felt from experience that he doubted what he ought to have believed. One night, as he was returning home at a late hour, from a meeting of Presbytery, and the customary dinner which followed, he was seized by the fairies, and carried aloft into the air. Through fields of ether and fleecy cloud he journeyed many a mile, descrying the earth far distant below him, and no bigger than a nut-shell. Being thus sufficiently convinced of the reality of their existence, they let him down at the door of his own house, where he afterwards often recited to the wondering circle, the marvellous tale of his adventure. Some people will believe that " spirits " of a different sort had a little to do with the worthy minister's conviction, and that his " ain gude grey mare " had more to do with bringing him to his own door than the fairies

It is difficult to describe a Hallowe'en as enjoyed by a family circle in olden times. An eye-witness has given the following account of it :—" When I entered the house, the tide of enjoyment was rolling on in full career. I listened and thought I heard an unusual noise in the apartment immediately above. The noise, however, was by no means of an alarming kind. It appeared to be the obstreperous romping of a parcel of youngsters. I found that the ladies of the house had brought together a number of young friends to burn nuts and duck for apples. I ascertained that previous to my appearance, they had already gone through the greater part of the ceremonies of the evening. They had pulled stocks, burnt nuts, and were now collected with earnest and somewhat awe-stricken faces, round a table on which stood two or three wine-glasses full of pure water. They were, in fact, about to commence the ceremony of dropping the egg—a ceremony which is performed by puncturing a fresh egg with a pin, when the person whose destiny is to be read holds it over a glass of pure water, into which he allows a few drops from the egg to fall. The glass is then held up to the candle, and some important event in the future life of the inquirer is found exhibited hieroglyphically in the glass,—the egg droppings assuming an endless variety of shapes, in which the skilful in these matters discover a resemblance to things, which, by association, clearly point out coming circumstances and events. All this was done by an old, weird sybil, who had been invited for the special purpose of reading to the young folks the various signs and indications of this privileged right. We all tried our fortunes after the most approved manner of egg-dropping, by the direction of the withered sybil already alluded to, and who, indeed, looked the very 'beau ideal' of a witch, or fortune-teller of coming events. She was old, shrivelled, and haggard—had a shrill, sharp voice, and was withal marvellously. loquacious. She seemed to be deeply in earnest, and to be strongly impressed with the solemnities which were going forward, and was more than once highly displeased with what she considered our irreverence for these matters, and the unbecoming and ill-timed levity with which we heard each other's fortunes foretold. We had all now tried our luck, with various results, but there was one young gentleman, who, I thought, seemed rather disinclined to go through the ceremony—and indeed, he finally endeavoured to back out altogether by a forced joke. We all urged him on, however, and at length fairly drove him to the experiment. 'Come awa, come awa, my bonny man,—excuse me for speaking that way, but ye ken I've kent ye sin ye was a bairn, and hae dandled ye mony a time on my knee. Come awa, and lat's see what luck is to be yours. I'm sure it'll be gowd in goppins, and true love to brook it—a bonnie lady wi' a bonnier tocher.' Whilst the old woman was speaking, the youth, having advanced close to the table, was in the act of dropping, with rather an unsteady hand, the egg into the glass. This done: 'Here Janet,' he said, with an affected laugh, and at the same time handing the glass to her across the table—' Now, give me all the good things of this life, let not one be awanting on your peril.' Well, all awaited in silence the announcement of our friend's future fortune, as we felt a degree of interest, nay of awe, stealing in upon us, which gradually allayed the light spirit with which we had entered the apartment. The old woman had now gently raised the glass between her eye and the candle, and having peered through it for a second—' Eh! gude guide us, Sirs,' she exclaimed, 'Gude guide us, what's this we hae here; but it canna be, it canna be, let me see,' and she looked with an increased intensity at the fatal signs. 'Ay! ay !' she said again, 'it's but owre true, my bairn, my bairn,' she added, and laying down the glass on the table. ' Are ye sure it was your glass ye gae me ?' 'Sure enough, Janet, sure enough, what's all this fuss about ?' 'What is it, Janet, what is't, what is't ?' now burst from both old and young, all being wound up to a pitch of the most intense interest to know what was that fate which Janet's expressions so particularly and fearfully hinted at. 'I insist on knowing,' said the young gentleman, striking his hand on the table with a sort of good-natured energy, for he affected to be laughing at the time. ' I insist upon it,' he said, 'for the edification of all present. Come then, Janet, any thing you like short of premature death and ruin, and crossed love.' ' But it's short o' neither, my bairn ! Alas ! it's short o' neither,' said the old woman gravely and seriously. 'It's indeed short o' neither—there's a winding sheet there wi' a fearful rent in it, and that ye ken, betokens a violent death ; there's a'—here, perceiving that things were getting rather serious, I suddenly burst in with an affected shout of hilarity, overturned the glass, talked loudly and obstreperously, and insisted upon our adjourning to the apartment we had left. So, with a wild, but assumed glee, we hurriedly descended to the room below.

"We endeavoured to enjoy ourselves, but still a weight seemed to have been laid upon the spirits of us all, which nothing could remove. We all felt the absurdity of permitting such a frivolous circumstance as the egg-dropping to depress us, but we could not hide from ourselves the fact that it had depressed us, and more particularly so, as our excellent host—a kind-hearted youth of twenty-three—had evidently taken the sybil's vaticinations too severely to heart. Under this feeling, and after our kind host had made such ineffectual attempts to restore the gaiety of the evening, the party broke up, each went his own way, and I retired to bed. 'Confound that old hag,' said my friend, just as I was about to part with him for the night ; 'confound her, she has spoiled our evening's enjoyment with her nonsense. Wasn't it evident,' he said, 'that our friends were damped by the fooleries up-stairs ?' I said, avoiding a direct answer, 'that we had spent a very pleasant night, and if there was any feeling of the kind he alluded to, a night's sleep would entirely remove it.' I met my friend and his aunts next morning at breakfast, where he more than once alluded to the circumstance during our meal ; and indeed fairly allowed that, in despite of the contempt with which he viewed such things, he could not help the idea of the rent winding-sheet still retaining its hold on his imagination.

" It will serve no purpose to relate the history of this unfortunate youth. The impression of the old hag's prediction never left him, but increased in intensity as some years passed on. He became addicted to intemperate habits, and utterly heedless of his worldly affairs. He squandered his patrimonial estate, and ruined his aged aunts, who lived with him. Ultimately, he wandered in beggary to a neighbouring city, and frequented the lowest haunts of dissipation, where he was found by a friend, who had gone in search of him, but found exactly an hour after he had swallowed a vial of laudanum. He opened his eyes, and knew his friend, who had just procured a surgeon ; but all in vain. His last words were—' Oh ! the winding sheet ; the rent winding-sheet !' and in less than two hours, he gently expired."

There are instances of the minds of some having been unhinged through the influence of undue credulity in certain practices of this nature. It has frequently happened besides, that personal injury has been inflicted, unintentionally no doubt, by the frolics and fooleries of that evening. The throwing of cabbage runts and large round turnips down the "lums," or chimneys of the cottars' dwellings, have often struck violently upon the family group around the cosy ingle, and inflicted serious injuries. The ceremony of throwing the clue of blue yarn into the pit of the kiln is one that has been attended with unhappy results. Kilns for drying corn are generally erected in lonely places, apart from the other dwellings, owing to their liability to catch fire. On the other hand, the kiln-logies or pits, are dreary, dark, deep receptacles, of circular form, narrow below and wide above, like hollow cones inverted. During the romping frivolities of the domestic circle in performing as many of the games as they can, lots are cast as to the maiden who must resort to the kiln at the dark hour of midnight, with her clue of blue thread in her hand, to meet with her sweetheart, or to hear his name. The selected "lass" must go, and go alone, however dark and stormy the night. It requires no small fortitude to enter the damp, dark kiln, to climb to the upper ridge of the kiln-logie, and to sit in that weird position in utter darkness. By this time, however, a number of the young men, unknown to the girl, had resorted to the kiln, and concealed themselves in and around the place. The girl, with palpitating heart cast her clue in to the kiln-logie, retaining the end of the thread in her hand, and exclaiming, with tremulous voice, "Co e sud th'air ceann mo ròpain ?' (Who is there at the end of my rope or thread?) Some of the youths, hidden in the kiln, would enter the aperture or fire-place below, lay hold of the clue in the pit, and cry with a feigned-unnatural voice, "I am here, what want ye with me?" "Who art thou, and what thy name, bold swain ?" The replies to this query were various. Some said that they were the girl's sweetheart, others, that they were wizards or beings of the supernatural order. Some even wickedly feigned to be the prince of darkness, when the preconcerted shrieking and howling of the hidden fellows so terrified the trembling young female above, as to render her a helpless maniac for life.

SACRED WELLS AND LOCHS.—The veneration that has been paid for ages to "Sacred Wells," and the confidence placed in their charms all over the kingdom for the curing of diseases, both mental and bodily, falls next to be noticed. It appears of old that if a well had a peculiar situation, if its waters were bright and clear, it was dedicated to some tutelary saint, by honouring it with his name. Thus we have St. Fillan's, St. Conel's, St. Catherine's, St. Bernard's, St. Cuthbert's wells, and a host of others in Scotland. We have hundreds of holy wells in England, such as St. Chad's, St. John's, St. Mary's, St. Madern's wells, all remarkable for something. We have St. Winifred's holy well in Flintshire, the most famous in the three kindgoms, at whose shrine Geraldus Cambrensis offered his devotions in the twelfth century. The vast majority of holy wells were frequented for any disease, while some wells were visited for special ailments, for the cure of which they had been celebrated. St. Tegla's well was patronised by sufferers from the falling sickness ; St. John's, Balmanno, Kincardineshire, by rickety children, and sore eyes. The waters of Trinity Gask, Perthshire, will render all baptised therein proof against every plague. In the Island of St. Kilda there are two wells— " Tobar nam buadh " (the spring of virtues), celebrated for deafness, and "Tobar a' chleirich " (the clerk's well)—which, though covered twice a day by the sea, never becomes brackish.  At Kirkden, in Angus, there is a well said to cure all sores, by mere washing, after the applications of skilled physicians had proved ineffectual.  But by far the most interesting wells in this country are those formerly resorted to for the cure of insanity.  Of these may be mentioned St. Fillan's well, near Tyndrum, Perthshire, as well as St. Nun's celebrated fountain in Cornwall.  The curing process at St. Fillan's may be described as a specimen.  The lunatics were first plunged into the water, wherein they were tumbled and tossed about rather roughly.  They were then carried into the adjacent Chapel of St. Fillan's and there secured with ropes, tied in a special way.  A celebrated bell, which has a history of its own, was then placed with great solemnity on the patient's head.  There the poor creature was left all night alone in the dreary chapel, and, if in the morning he was found unloosed, hopes were entertained that he would recover his reason, but the case was hopeless if found still in his bonds.  Very frequently the patients were released from the bonds and tormentors by death, caused by the cold, and all the cruelties inflicted upon them.  St. Catherine's well, near Edinburgh, was regarded in olden times with great awe, because there appeared a black substance on its surface which could be set on fire.  This dark-looking, greasy substance or oil, was supposed to proceed from the strata of coal underneath, and it was believed to cure all sorts of cutaneous diseases.  In the north end of Skye, and a little beneath the towering cliffs of the far-famed Quiraing, there is a conflux of pure, fresh-water springs, which form a small elliptical pond of considerable depth.  It is a beautiful spot, pleasantly hemmed in with shrubs and bushes.  It is called "Loch Sianta," or the Holy Lake.  Owing to the natural beauty of this little Hebridean Siloam, the natives conceived it to be favoured with its divinity, to whom, in the days of darkness and superstition, they were extremely punctual in making offerings of various kinds. Invalids resorted thither, drank of its waters, washed themselves therein, and received cures thereby for their mental and bodily ailments. These superstitions have, however, long ceased, and Loch Sianta, though beautiful as ever, has lost its ancient charms in this more enlightened age. On the first Sunday of May (old style) the well at "Creagag" or Craigie, in Munlochy Bay, was believed to possess powerful charms against diseases, witchcraft, fairies and such like. For weeks before the time, old and young prepared for their pilgrimage to this well. All behoved to bring their offerings. Coloured threads and rags of cloth were brought in thousands, and hung upon the rocks and brushwood, as propitiatory gifts to the saint of the healing waters. Even in St. Kilda the divinities of "Tobar nam buadh" and "Tobar a' chleirich" had to be propitiated by offerings, in the shape of shells, pins, needles, pebbles, coins, or rags, otherwise their tutelary saint would be inexorable. So common, indeed, was this habit, that at the Rug-well, near Newcastle, the shrubs and bushes near the spring were densely covered with rags. And many of my readers are old enough to have seen crowds of the good citizens of the Highland Capital flocking on a May morn eastward to the well at Culloden to taste of its waters, and to cover with their offerings of rags the branches of the surrounding trees. There is a place beyond Kessock Ferry, near the point of Kilmuir, called "Craigie-How," where there is a cave close to the sea-beach. In this cave a little water falls down from the roof in drops on the stones below. These drops are to this day considered a complete cure for deafness, if properly applied. The patient lies down, and lays his head on the flags, and lets the water fall first into the one ear and then into the other. After some formalities are gone through, the patient rises, and the deafness is believed to be gone !

Loch Maree also has its Sacred well. The scenery of this part of Gairloch, in Ross-shire, is unsurpassed, and perhaps rarely, if at all equalled, by that of any other quarter of the kingdom. The mountains which surround Loch Maree are of great height, and of beautifully characterised outline. Their lofty, jagged, serrated peaks, like Macbeth's witches, " so withered and so wild in their attire," present the finest specimens of the grand and picturesque to be met with anywhere. The gigantic Slioch (Sliabhach) towering to a height of more than 4000 feet, is seen from afar, even from the remotest of the Northern Hebrides. Within the bosom of these mountains lies enshrined the far-famed Loch Maree, with its many wooded islets, so varied in size and so different in appearance. About twenty-seven of these lie in a cluster near the middle of the lake (opposite the Loch Maree Hotel), which is eighteen miles in length, and two in average breadth.

Dr. M'Culloch writes—" It was with some difficulty that we explored our way through the labyrinth of Islands in the centre of this lake ; as they are little raised above the water, and covered with scattered firs, and thickets of birch, alder, and holly, while they are separated by narrow and tortuous channels." The scene indeed, is so grand, wild, and fantastic, that words are at fault to describe it. Some years ago it was visited by tourists, whose admiration of it cannot be better expressed than in their own words. " When this majestic scene first burst upon our view, the effect was as surprising and enchanting, as it was unexpected. The lake sparkled bright in the evening sun. The lofty mountains were, at their summits, tinged with his golden rays, while in the hollows, and nearer their base, they were wreathed in

mist and light clouds.   The effect of this was to increase to
a prodigious degree, the apparent height of the mountains,
to make every hollow on their rugged sides, seem a deep
and inaccessible glen, and to enlarge to an almost immeasur-
able extent the lake, and the hills which rose at its extreme
distance.   It was altogether a scene of enchantment never
to be forgotten.   The white piqued summits of the File-
Mountain sparkled like the spires and turrets of an emerald
palace, the work of some eastern magician, or of the genii
of Arabian romance, and forming a splendid contrast to the
dark and rugged Slioch, which rises from the opposite side
of the lake !"

It is by no means surprising that Superstition, in her
fantastic freaks, should have, in ages long byegone, selected
this weird locality for the manifestation of not a few of her
favourite protegés.

This superb sheet of water, from its almost unfathomable
depth and other dimensions, furnished a befitting receptacle
for brownies, water-horses, uruisgean, kelpies, and such like,
while one of the islets of this beautiful lake became the arena
of various superstitious practices, and of curing therewith
some of the most inveterate diseases.   The largest of these
Islands are Eilean Suthain (St. Swithan's Isle), Eilean
Ruairidh Mhoir, and Eilean Ruairidh Bhig.   Eilean Maree
is the most celebrated, and was, as some think, dedicated
to the Virgin Mary ; others assert that it is named after St.
Malrube ; but more probably it is called after a Prince, or
petty King who occupied the Island—is, in short, "Loch-ma-
Righ," or Loch of my King.   It has a burying-ground with
tombstones bearing inscriptions and hieroglyphical figures,
which cannot now be deciphered.   There is in the Island
also a Sacred Well, in which, as in the pool of St. Fillan's,
lunatics were plunged and healed, and, in short, all manner

of diseases cured.   Around this sacred spot the usual ob-
lations were made to the tutelary saint, and coins of every
descriptions stuck into a tree that grew out of the bank.
The sacred water of this well was deemed so effectual in
curing the insane, that they were brought to it from the
remotest quarters of the north.   The treatment they received
was no doubt somewhat severe.   Before they drank of its
waters, it was reckoned indispensable to the permanency of
their cure, that they should be dragged at the stern of a
boat twice round the Island, pulled by a rope made of horse-
hair, fastened under their arms and around their shoulders.
They were then dipped in the well, and drank of its
water.

Her Gracious Majesty, Queen Victoria, recently paid a
visit to this romantic district, and held a religious service on
the Island.   In commemoration of this welcome visit she
has been pleased to sanction a memorial inscription, by the
proprietor of Gairloch, on a large stone opposite the Loch
Maree Hotel, in which she took up her abode.   In this
manner our beloved sovereign, whose eye is always keen to
observe, whose taste is exquisite to admire, and whose
sensibility is great to appreciate all that is grand and beautiful in Nature's workmanship, has conferred a lasting honour
on the true-hearted Highland Chief, Sir Kenneth S. Mackenzie, Baronet ; on his loyal and delighted tenantry ; as
well as on his romantic property in Gairloch.

It may be remarked that there is hardly a lake, or peren-
nial fountain in Scotland of any magnitude, but has certain
traditional stories connected with it, bearing reference to
something wild or supernatural.   The celebrated Hugh
Miller relates the following regarding the " Fiddler's Well,"
near Cromarty :—" There is a little path which, in the
eastern part of the parish, goes winding over rock and stone

along the edge of a range of low-browed precipices, till it reaches a fine spring of limpid water, that comes gushing out of the side of a bank, covered with moss and daises. This beautiful spring has been known to the people of the town, for a century and more, by the name of Fiddler's Well. Its waters are said to be medicinal; and there is a tradition still preserved, of the circumstance through which its virtues were first discovered, and to which it owes its name. Two young men of the place, who were much attached to each other, were seized at nearly the same time by consumption. In one the progress of the disease was rapid; he died two short months after he was attacked by it; while the other, though wasted almost to a shadow, had yet strength enough left to follow the corpse of his companion to the grave. The surname of the survivor was Fiddler, a name still common among the seafaring men of the town. On the evening of the interment, he felt oppressed and unhappy, his imagination was haunted by a thousand feverish shapes of open graves, with bones smouldering round their edges, and of coffins with the lids displaced; and after he had fallen asleep, the images, which were still the same, became more grissly and horrible. Towards morning, however, they had all vanished; and he dreamed that he was walking alone by the sea-shore in a clear beautiful day in summer. Suddenly, as he thought, some person stepped up behind, and whispered into his ear, in the voice of his deceased companion, 'Go on, Willie, I shall meet you at Stormy'. There is a rock in the neighbourhood of Fiddler's Well, so called from the violence with which the sea beats against it, when the wind blows strongly from the east. On hearing the voice, he turned round, and seeing no one, he went on as he thought, to the place named, in the hope of meeting with his friend, and sat down on a bank to wait for his coming; but he waited long, lonely and dejected; and then remembering that he for whom he waited was dead, he burst into tears. At this moment, a large field-bee came humming from the west, and began to fly round his head. He raised his hand to brush it away; it widened its circle, and then came humming in to his ear as before. He raised his hand a second time, but the bee could not be scared off; it hummed ceaselessly round and round him, until at length its murmurings seemed to be fashioned into words, articulated in the voice of his deceased companion. ' Dig, Willie, and drink,' it said, ' Dig, Willie, and drink.' He, accordingly, set himself to dig, and no sooner had he torn a sod out of the bank, than a spring of clear water gushed from the hollow; and the bee, taking a wider circle, and humming in a voice of triumph that seemed to emulate the sound of a trumpet, flew away. He looked after it, but as he looked, the images of his dream began to mingle with those of the waking world; the scenery of the hill seemed obscured by a dark cloud, in the centre of which there glimmered a faint light; the rocks, the sea, the long declivity faded into the cloud; and turning round, he saw only a dark apartment, and the first beams of morning shining in at the window. He rose, and after digging the well, drank of the water, and recovered. And its virtues are still celebrated; for though the water be only simple water, it must be drunk in the morning, and as it gushes out of the bank; and with pure air, exercise, and early rising for its auxiliaries, it continues to work cures." *

*Since this was first published, the late Alexander Fraser, Registrar, Inverness, a well-known Northern Antiquarian, wrote four full and most interesting papers, entitled, *Northern Folk-lore on Wells and Water; with an Account of some interesting Wells in the neighbourhood of Inverness and the North*, which appeared in the *Celtic Magazine*, Vol. III., pp. 348, 370, 419, and 456.

It has been remarked, that almost all our lakes, fountains, pools, waterfalls, rocky crevices, and caves, have been tenanted, by superstition, with water-horses, kelpies, uruisgean, and brownies.  Of this there are many instances in the Highland districts of Perthshire, which are now made classic ground by the magic pen of the author of Waverley.  Beinn Venue is a lofty mountain which rises from the south-east shore of Loch Katrine.  The celebrated " Coir-nan-Uruisgean," or Goblin's Cave, is situated at its base.  It is guarded by precipitous rocks, which lie strewed in immense fragments on every side, and this well-defended corrie or cave, affords a safe asylum for foxes, badgers, and wild-cats ; as also one equally safe, if the natives be credited, for the goblins, kelpies, and uruisgean.  The uruisgean are, in short, no strangers in various quarters of Perthshire, as well as in most parts of the Highlands.  Dr. Graham says that they are " a sort of lubberly supernaturals, who could be gained over by kind attention, to perform the drudgery of the farm ; and it was believed that many Highland families had some of the order so tamed, as to become attached to them".  Sir Walter Scott states that " tradition has ascribed to the uruisgean, a figure between a goat and a man ; in short, however much the classical reader may be startled, precisely that of a Grecian Satyr."

It is related of an honest farmer's wife in Glenlyon, that. one wet morning, as the decent matron was in the act of making the porridge for the family breakfast, she had an unexpected visit from an " uruisg," who came in quite unceremoniously, cold, dripping with rain, and squatted herself close by the cheering fire.  There the huge, slippery-skinned, uncouth monster lay, enjoying the genial warmth, but awkwardly impeding the worthy good-wife from cooking the family meal.  Sadly annoyed at the monster's impertinence, the good old lady lifted a ladleful of the boiling beverage from the pot on the fire, and poured it on the sides and thighs of her unwelcome guest, on which, the creature arose suddenly, darted off in a moment, upsetting tables and chairs, and exclaiming in pure Gaelic :—

> Ochan ! loisg thu mi, chràidh thu mi,
> Led' bhrochan teth, tana, gu'n stà ;
> Ach fhad's bhios uisg' ann an Liobhain,
> Cha chriochnaich do pheanas gu bràth.
>     A' Chaillich gu'n mhodh, is gu'n nair
>     'S tu chiurr mi gu goirt, is gu searbh,
>     Ach thig mi le armachd gu'n dàil,
>     Is cuiream gu bàs thu gu dearbh !

We ought to learn one lesson from this subject—gratitude to the Great Ruler, because we live in more favourable circumstances, and under the light and liberty of a preached Gospel. The press and the pulpit have now opened the eyes of men; the schoolmaster is abroad; and many superstitions by which past ages have been deluded have greatly vanished before the pure light of evangelic truth. In many quarters of the world they have disappeared before the lustre of that revelation which has brought the truth of immortality to light, and which impresses the imagination of man with truer notions and simpler imagery. We cannot but admire the dauntless courage of Paul when he boldly faced the Epicurean and stoic philosophers—when " he stood in the midst of Mars' Hill, and said, Ye men of Athens, I perceive that in all things ye are too superstitious". There he met a people, the most distinguished for the wisdom of their political constitution, for the brilliancy of their achievements, for the extent and variety of their learning, and for the refinement of their manners ; yet a people who, amid all their glory and renown, were ignorant of the true God, and lived the blind and deluded victims of the grossest idolatry and superstition.

**THE END.**

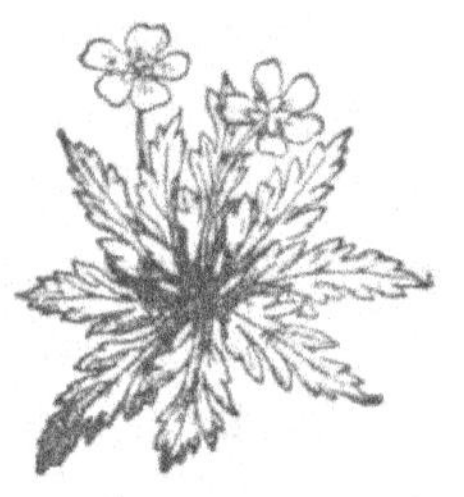



Munro & Jamieson, Stirling.

www.ingramcontent.com/pod-product-compliance
Lightning Source LLC
Chambersburg PA
CBHW081743280726
48660CB00021B/3408